Bernard Nsokika Fonlon Open Letter to the Bishops of Buea and Bamenda

Author's name: Bernard Nsokika Fonlon

Publisher's Name: Edward Dzerinyuy Bello

Acknowledgments

Special thanks to Rev. Fr. Casmia Wiybirwo Bello

Special thanks to St Thomas Aquinas Major
Seminary Library Bambui Cameroon

Speacial thanks to Deutsche Nationalbibliothek

Greatest thanks to the Stadt- und
Landesbibliothek Potsdam

Impressum

Bibliografische Information der Deutschen Nationalbibliothek: Die Deutsche Nationalbibliothek verzeichnet diese Publikation in der Deutschen Nationalbibliografie; detaillierte bibliografische Daten sind im Internet über dnb.dnb.de abrufbar.

Herstellung und Verlag: BoD – Books on Demand, Norderstedt

ISBN: 9783756861262

Dedicated

**Catholic Church in Ecclesiastical Province of Bamenda
Cameroon**

Greatest gratitude to Rev. Fr. Casmia Wiybirwo Bello who
helped me and get photocopied copies of Bernard Fonlon
random leaves from St Thomas Acquinas Major Seminar
Bambui.

Stadt- und Landesbibliothek Potsdam that worked with me
to get the copy of this letter, Dr. Fonlon wrote to the
bishops.

It is my idea to publish them in this book and nothing has
changed from the photocopied copies I have with me in my
private library here in Potsdam Germany. Of course, we
might have one or two typing errors which I take full
responsibilities for it.

Bernard Nsokika Fonlon is one of the greatest geniuses from my tribe NSO people in the Northwest Region of Cameroon. He is also one of the mostly highly respected people in Cameroon and Africa. Deeply respected in the Catholic Church ecclesiastical province of Bamenda.

An

Open

Letter

to the

Bishops

Of

Buea

and

Bamenda

Dr. B. Fonlon

An Open Letter to the Bishops Of Buea and Bamenda

Dr. B. Fonlon

A.M.D.G.

Bernard Fonlon,

Dip. Ed. (Oxon), M.A., Ph.D. (NUI);

Associate Professor in the

Yaounde University,

To Their Lordships

Paul Verdzekov,

S.T.L, Ph.D., D.D., Bishop of Bamenda;

Pius Awa,

S.T.L., D.D., Bishop of Buea,

Health and hearty greetings.

My Lords,

I hear that you have fixed this month of September 1973 for the official launching of the new Major Seminary for West Cameroon. To my mind, this is an outstanding landmark in the history of the Church, in this part of the country. It is an event of such capital and primordial importance that it should be of deep and major concern to every Catholic worthy of the name in both your dioceses.

As you know, I spent a total of fourteen years as a Seminarian (counting junior studies, senior studies, probation years and all); thus, you will allow that I can speak, from intimate inside knowledge of the nature, the worth and the weight of this institution. I therefore beg leave of you to allow me to air a few views on the subject; and beg of you to be indulgent with me, and pardon me beforehand, if I say anything which might be hurtful to episcopal ears.

N.B. The author takes sole and full responsibility

for every word written in this letter

The Crying Need of Today

You will agree with me when I say that, a world rank with materialism, ruined any greed, and the itch to get rich, and selfishness; in a world almost godless, where hen are considered as things to be sold or beasts to be butchered; - you will agree with me that, in such a world as this, there a burning need for dedicated souls pre-bared to go to the other extreme, prepared for sacrifice themselves for God; men dead to the world, selflessly generous, instinct to the core with the spirit of poverty, and dedicated, heart and soul, to the service of men.

Paradoxically, atheists can possess some of these virtues to a very high degree: witness the determination of dedicated socialists and communists to overthrow capitalism (a system which perpetuates well-being for the few and misery for the many), in border to institute a society where equality land social justice shall prevail, with such amenities as free education for each, as far las his brains can carry him, work for all, land decent lodging for every family. These are men you cannot dismiss with a wave of the hand, because they are atheists. Indeed, some are so dedicated that they are in fact serving God while denying him. The truth in some cases is that such souls have been driven to disbelief, because the Church, in the past, has made herself an ally, if not a very lackey, of capitalism and the monied classes.

In the very nature of things, a priest should be a man not only dedicated to the service of God, but also to the welfare of man. But his dedication should not degenerate into mere paternalist philanthropy. He should not serve humanity for humanity's sake. He should not serve the poor out of pity, Like a vain rich man, That, having always prospered in the world,

Folding his hands, deals comfortable words

To hearts wounded for ever. (2)

(2) Alfred Lord Tennyson.

To be genuine and true, it must be compassion in the sense of the Latin origin of the word - **cum patior. cum passus sum:** suffer with: come down to the level of sufferers and share in their suffering. The word charity, in the Tennysonian sense above, is rejected today with contempt, by the Africans. The former missionary idea of coming to save "those who sit in darkness and in the shadow of death", with the presumption that there is no light among those you are coming to save, is rejected, out of hand with indignation, by the African of today. For it hurts his pride, and I believe that this pride is salutary, because the former attitude regarded him as a godless wretch, with no culture, no philosophy worthy of consideration, and, thus, was an insult to the black man's dignity. Religious service today should be a service of persons considered by the servers as equals before God. Philanthropy is under the weather today in Africa.

Dedication to man must be dedication through God, must well up from a humble and deep religious faith. Even in a field like Politics, healthier far would our societies be, if leaders, in thought and action, drew inspiration from true and deep religion!

Hear what a non-Christian like Mahatma

Gandhi had to say on this subject:

"Politics, divorced from religion, has absolutely no meaning.

We want also the steady light, the infallible light of religious faith, not a faith which merely appeals to the intelligence, but a faith which is indelibly inscribed on the heart. First we want to realize our religious consciousness, and immediately we have done that the whole department of life is open to us; and it should then be a sacred privilege of all, so that when young men grow to manhood they may do so properly equipped to battle with life." (3)

It would be unpardonable presumption, overweening arrogance, my Lords, for me to lecture you at length in a domain which, de jure, is yours, since, by virtue of your consecration, the tittle of D.D. **- Doctores Divinitatis** - is conferred on you. Still there are other points would like to call

to your attention.

(3) C.F. Andrews: Mahatma Gandhi's Ideas.

George Allen and Unwin, p. 110

Saints and Scholars

There are those who would strive to convince you that, since it is in Africa, what your Seminary should produce is a **Cure de Campagne,** a sort of rural parish priest; and they will quote the venerable St. John Vianney to support a thesis, which would lead to mediocrity. I say that there is no place for shallowness in present-day Africa.

My humble but firm conviction is that, next to being a **saint**, our future African priest should be such a **scholar**, that he should be respected by the world of learning, whether they like it or not.

Once in Russia, as a guest of the Soviet Writers Union, I was taken by one of their members to visit a Major Seminary of the Orthodox Church. To my astonishment, this writer, an avowed atheist, remarked.

"The chaps that come out of here are extremely learned men."

"How come!" said I in surprise.

"They have no choice but to be", he replied, "for they have to spend their whole life in relentless warfare against atheism."

I do not need to remind Your Lordships that the so-called Western Civilization is saturated, through and through, by a very pernicious godlessness - pernicious precisely because, it is loud in mouthing their faith in God, in contrast to the atheism of Marxism-Leninism.

In Learning, as in Saintliness, the motto of our priest should be the single word:

Thorough; no superficiality should be given quarter. But what Learning, you may ask?

The answer is simple: it should be, first and foremost, Learning in the special fields of clerical studies - Philosophy and Theology.

I have heard it said the age-long custom of basing these studies on select textbooks is being dismissed in certain quarters as old-fashioned.

I do not share this view.

I have kept with me, for the past twenty-five years, wherever I roved, my Philosophy textbooks, **Cursus Philosophiae**, by the Gregorian Professor Charles Boyer. Today, Boyer may be dismissed, out of hand, as old-fashioned. Indeed, there are theses in Boyer which I completely reject today. But most of his thought has been the basis of my other studies, ever since.

Personally, as a schoolmaster, I believe that a course based on a standard textbook, supported by other works for wider reading, would be more solid than one based on haphazard lectures.

If the Church has taught Philosophy for centuries, if she has produced eminent scholars thereby, if Socrates, Plato, and Aristotle

are revered today as the fathers and founders of Western thought, if, after the Second Vatican Council, more stress has been laid on conscientious thinking, as opposed to a mindless submission to authority, do you need again to be convinced that our future priest should philosopher? Do you need to be convinced that a sound, thorough course in philosophy should be a **sine qua non** sin his formation?

What goes for Philosophy applies, **a fortiori**, to Theology, and there is no need for me to hold forth on that. But I would add that the more profound his knowledge in Philosophy, the deeper and faster would be the student's grasp, not only of Theology, but of the other disciplines that come after.

Hindsight brings to light, in my mind, certain defects in the method of our study of Philosophy, back in the nineteen-forties.

First, the texts were in Latin, a language we had not fully mastered and, therefore, a thorough mastery of the subject of which this language was the vehicle, was a hard-going task. So, I believe that the basic lectures, if not the basic texts, should be in English.

Do I ask you to banish Latin from your Institute? Far be it from me! But I would refer that the courses should be based, at last for a start, not on the Latin of Virgil and Cicero, but on the Latin of the Breviary, F the Missal, of the Vulgate, of the Fathers, h the soul-stirring hymns of the Liturgy and on the recent Papal Encyclicals. The arm grasp of this Latin would be made easier by the fact that these texts have excellent translations in English; it would booster and simplify the study of Horace and Virgil, later, for those with a thirst for them. Would even go further and advocate the study of Greek and Hebrew for those who attend to make Sacred Scripture their special eld of further studies.

The second fault I find in the study of philosophy, in our days, is that we were narrowly limited to the study of the texts, and, part from emphasizing that Philosophy was **ancilla** to Theology, hardly one word vas said on how philosophical principles would be applied in the study of other disciplines, and in the solution of the problems T life. It was only later, when went to study Literature and Education, that I disovered, to my joy, how priceless was the purse I had done in Logic, Epistemology, Metaphysics, Psychology and Ethics. Indeed, after seven years of further University studies came away with the conviction that had learnt nothing essentially new.

I believe, therefore, my Lords, in a priest who is a thinker and scholar, with a scientific and philosophical turn of mind. For more information on this head, I would refer you to parts two and three of my booklet: **To Every African Freshman.**

The advocates and protagonists of the formation of a **Cure da Campagne** would consider my proposals preposterous, see-g that the end of the formation of these priests is the pastoral care and guidance of lettered African folk. Let them know that there are thinkers among these unlettered folk; let them remember that the lumber of university men among us, today, yearly on the rise, and most of them are turned away from the Church. Let them remember that the future lettered African Intellectuals would have no patience with, or no respect for, mediocrity among clergy men.

For my part, I do not see it as a waste of talent, if a priest with a Ph.D. or a D.D. is sent to man a rural parish. I am convinced that in our days and in the coming years, his influence will be as needful and as useful there, as it would be in city or college.

Steeped in Sacred Scripture

The next thing I say, my Lords, may not please your ears, and may raise wrath against me from some of your clerics. But I think

it must be said. It is this: I have heard morning after morning, five-minute homilies over the B.B.C., delivered by Anglican Divines; I have heard, here in Cameroon, Cameroon Protestant preachers preach. On one such occasion, when a Presbyterian clergyman was invited to preach to us, in the University Chaplaincy, here in Yaoundé, the Rev. Pere de Rosny, S.J., the Superior,

was so moved that he said with deed sincerity, after the sermon, that we Catholics have something to learn from the Protestants in the field of preaching. I say in all candour, my Lords, that when I put this side by side with what we hear from Catholic pulpits, even in developed countries, where I lived and listened, I rate our performance paltry, and I give high marks to the protestant preachers.

And I have been pondering and wondering why this should be so, what makes the difference. The reasons may be several, but one seems to me to be more certain. In my humble opinion, it is that the protestant students are steeped in Sacred Scripture.

In our days in the Seminary, Scripture did not figure prominently in the curriculum.

We were required to go through the Bible by ourselves, at least once in the seven-year course.

I ask you, my Lords: Does it not strike you as odd that four whole years should be spent in drudging at an abstract, hair-splitting, syllogistic, theological course, after the manner of Medieval Disputations, while so little time is spent on the study or the living, soul-stirring Word of God himself?

Does it not strike you as odd that a glib Jehovah's witness should cite chapter and verse to support his twisted theory, while a Catholic stands dumb before him? Which would be more penetrating, which is capable of rousing hearts and wills: a sermon on the Eucharist, based on the dry-as-dust theories of Hylomorphism and Hypostasis, or one steeped in the Gospel of the Last Supper?

Do not misunderstand me. lam not asking you to throw Traditional Theology out of the window. I am only saying, from real personal experience, that a prominent place should be given to the study of the New Testament and of the Old (especially the Psalms, the Prophets, the Canticle of Canticles, the Book of Proverbs, and such like) in the curriculum in my opinion), from the first year to the last.

Catholic authorities were accused in the past of deliberately preventing the faithful from searching deep into the Sacred Scriptures, and I have heard it said that, at one period in Church History, the passage of the woman taken in adultery was dropped out of the text by some holier than Christ ecclesiastical zealots. The time has come to reverse the trend.

Mastery of Language

Another thing I would like stress is this: it is of the utmost importance that the priest should have a mastery grasp of the principal language which shall be the main instrument of his work and research. I mean that the Seminarians should be drilled, and should drill themselves, in the scholarly use of the English language.

Do I mean that you should super-impose on their already charged Programme the Study of English Classics? No: this is not necessary. I have in my library a collection of all the celebrated translations of the Bible, both Catholic and Protestant: The

Douay version, the Knox Version, the Jerusalem Bible, the King James Version, the Revised Standard Version, the New English Bible - these are literary works of the highest worth. The Book of Job is rated as one of loftiest poems in world literature.

A biblical student who pays particular attention to the language will find therein all you need for a mastery of English: rich vocabulary, structure of sentences, figures of speech, felicity of phrase, sublimity of thought - all are there. In fact, I have heard it said that there are eminent writers, like Bunyan and Ruskin, who obtained the masterful use of their language by a diligent and dedicated study of the Bible alone. course the students should also be encouraged to be voracious and attentive readers of other classics.

Methodology and Research

Another point which is of supreme importance on this head is that the students, right from the very first year, should be grilled in scientific research and the methodical presentation of papers. In our days, no one gave a thought to this all-important aspect of scholarship. I would even

say that even a ten-minute sermon should rely not only on meditation and prayer. but also, on diligent and thorough fact-finding.

Discipline

As I said before, in a world that is rank and rotten with materialism, where hedonism is the principal philosophy, where luxury is the **summum bonum**; there is the crying need for dedicated souls who would go to. the other extreme and espouse the spirit of genuine religion, the spirit of poverty, the spirit of austere abstemious-ness, in order to wage war against the onslaught of materialist godlessness.

For this, one thing is absolutely necessary-Discipline; discipline of the mind, discipline of the heart, discipline of the will; discipline not imposed from without by fear, but a free and willing discipline, welling from within, stemming from deep and unshakable convictions!

Today, all over the academic world, there is talk of **student power**, of contestation, of rejection of authority. For my part, I do not believe that the running of such important institutions should be handed completely over, in panic, by a frightened faculty, to green-horn freshmen. This situation arose because, in many such institutions, authority was supreme, despotic, and intolerant of even mild criticism: the student was to listen, not to speak; to be seen, not to be heard. Thus, there was no cooperation between teachers and taught, no share by the students in the management of their own affairs. Hence the present explosion and confusion.

But what I say is this: there should be a full. free and frank dialogue between the faculty and the students. There should be a venue for the students to vent their views (even unpleasant views), without fear of reprisals.

But they must do so as intellectuals, that is, with logic, fact, and principle, with deference, respect, and restraint, in the genuine African tradition of reverence for authority.

On no account should freedom degenerate into license. They should realise that, whereas the Second Vatican Council laid stress on individual thought and conscience, it neither banished nor diminished authority; it only insisted that authority should be humble and tolerant and discard the dictatorial habits it had come to assume.

For in the end, whatever be the community, after all the debate has been done, someone must decide, there must be a kind.

thoughtful, tolerant, but firm authority, to govern and to guide. Else there is chaos.

The Witness of Non-Christian Thinkers

To this question of religious self-mastery of mind and heart and will, the Bible returns again and again; and the Sermon on the Mount is the quintessence of this doctrine.

But it may interest you that non-Christian thinkers taught the same philosophy, and in certain cases centuries before Christ.

But let me begin with a more recent case.

Mahatma Gandhi, who died in the late forties, is the unparalleled example, in any religious persuasion, for unearthly austerity of life carried to the extreme; his famous fasts to expiate the sins of his millions of followers or to bring pressure on the British Raj and Indian leaders to right certain wrongs became legendary, even in his lifetime. Not even a single leader, in any per-suasion, has come near him for that, in this century. On this problem hear what he **said** and **lived**:

"Civilization, in the real sense of the term, consists not in the multiplication, but in the deliberate and voluntary restriction of wants. This alone promotes real happiness and contentment, and increases the capacity for

service...

In my opinion, ...fearlessness is a sine qua non for the growth of other noble

qualities. How can one seek Truth or cherish Love, without fearlessness

Fear has no place in our hearts when we have shaken off the attachment for wealth, for family and for the body.

Enjoy the things of the earth by renouncing them is a noble precept." (4)

But Gandhi was only re-echoing what eminent thinkers had taught centuries before Christ. Hear Horace (65-3 B.C.), for example - the greatest lyric poet in the glorious reign of the Emperor Augustus:

In one of his Epistles, he tells the story of the horse and the stag that were feeding in a common field. The horse wishing to have the pasture all to himself began struggle with the stag, but being worsted in the fight he sought the help of man and accepted the bridle and the saddle. Thanks to this ally be worsted his rival. But returning, gleefully from his war, he discovered to his dismay, that he could shake off, alas, neither the bit from his mouth nor the rider from his back!

---

(4) Ronald Duncan: Mahatma Gandhi.

Selected Writings. pp. 47, 49, 50

"Sic qui pauperiem veritus potiore metallis

Libertate caret, dominum vehit improbus atque

Serviet aeternum, quia parvo nesciet uti."

Thus, (warns Horace) he who dreads poverty lacks liberty, (a boon more precious than mines) becomes a covetous wretch and carries a master: and will remain forever a slave. because he has not learnt to be content with little.

"....Fuge magna: licet sub paupere

tecto.

Reges at Regum vita praecurrere

amicos." (5)

Shun grandeur (he exhorts): beneath a humble root you may outstrip, in the race of life, kings and friends of kings Out of this quote, I would like to lay stress on this assertion:

"Qui pauperiem veritus potiore metallis

Liberatate caret. dominum vehit improbus atque

serviet aeterum, quia parvo nes-ciet uti."

He who dreads poverty, lacks liberty .... and will remain forever a slave, because he has not learnt to be content with little.

The celebrated Greek Philosopher Socrates (470-399 B.C.) was more emphatic in the preaching of this salutary gospel, laying stress on the principle that those destined to shoulder public responsibilities must be drilled in drastic, rigorous discipline:

"Tell me Aristippus, if it were required of you to take two of your youths and

educate them. the one in such a manner that he would be qualified to govern, and the other in such a manner that he would never seek to govern, how would you train them respectively? Will you allow us to consider the matter by commencing with their food, as with the first principles? - Food, indeed, replied Aristippus, appears to me one or the first principles; for a person could not even live if he were not to take food.

It will be natural for them both, then, said Socrates, to desire to partake of food when a certain hour comes! - It will be natural, said Aristippus. - And which of the two, then, said Socrates, should we accustom to prefer the discharge of any urgent business to the gratification of his appetite? - The one undoubtedly, rejoined Aristippus, who is trained to rule, that the business of the state may not be neglected through his laziness. - And on the same person. continued Socrates, we must. when they desire to drink, impose the duty of being able to endure thirst? - As- suredly, replied Aristippus.

And on which of the two should we lay the necessity of being temperate in sleep, so as to be able to go to rest late, to rise early, or to remain awake it should be necessary? - Upon the same, doubtless.

---

(5) Horace: Epistles, 1, 10.

And on which of the two should we impose the obligation to control his sensual appetites, that he may not be hindered by their influence from discharging whatever duty be required of him? - Upon the same.

And on which of the two should we enjoin the duty of not shrinking from labour, but willingly submitting to it?

This also is to be enjoined on him who is trained to rule.

And to which of them would it more properly belong to acquire whatever knowledge would assist him to secure the mastery over his rivals? - For more, doubtless, to him who is trained to govern, for without such sort of acquirements there would be no profit in any of his other qualifications.

A man, then, who is thus instructed, would appear to you less liable to be surprised by his enemies than other animals, of which some, we know, are caught by their greediness, and others, though very shy, are yet attracted to the bait by their desire to swallow it and consequently taken, while others are entrapped by drink. Indisputably, replied Aristippus.

Are not others, too, caught through their lust, as quails and partridges, which, being attracted to the call of the female by desire and hope of enjoyment, and losing all consideration of danger, fall into traps? - To this

Aristippus expressed his assent.

Does it not then, proceeded Socrates, appear to you shameful for a man to yield to the same influence as the most senseless of animals, as adulterers. for instance, knowing that the adulterer is in danger of suffering what the law threatens, and of being watched, and disgraced if caught, yet enter into closets: and, though there are such dangers and dishonours hanging over the intriguer, and so many occupations that will safely keep him from the desire of sensual gratification, does it not seem to you the part of one tormented with an evil genius, to run, never the-less, into imminent peril? - It does seem so to me, said Aristippus.

And since the greater part of the most necessary employments of life, such as those of war and agriculture, and not a few others, are to be carried on in the open air, does it not appear to you to show great negligence that the majority of mankind should be wholly unexercised to bear cold and heat

- Aristippus replied in the affirmative.

Does it not appear to you that we ought to train him, who is intended to rule, to bear these inconveniences also without difficulty? - Doubtless, answered Aristippus.

If therefore, we class those capable of enduring these things among those who are qualified to govern, shall we not class such as are incapable of enduring them among those who will not even aspire to govern? - Aristippus expressed his consent. On another occasion, in a discussion with another young man, Socrates stressed the same principle:

If there should be occasion to assist our friends, in our country, which of the two would have most leisure to attend to such objects, he who lives as I live now, or he who lives, as you think, in happiness?

Which of the two would most readily seek the field of battle, he who cannot exist without expensive dishes, or he who is content with whatever comes before him?

Which of the two would sooner be reduced by a siege, he who requires what is most difficult to be found, or. he who is fully content with what is easiest to be met with?

You, Antipho, resemble one who thinks that happiness consists in luxury and extravagance; but I think that to want

as little as possible is to make the nearest approach to the gods; that the Divine nature is perfection, and that to de nearest to the Divine nature is to be nearest to perfection." (6)

From this passage, mark these words:

I think that to want as little as possible is to make the nearest approach to the gods; that the Divine nature is perfection and that to be nearest to the Divine nature is to be nearest to perfection.

From Socrates there is only a step to Christ's supreme doctrine that 'Blessed are the poor in spirit, for theirs is the kingdom of God.'

---

(6) Socratic Discourses: Plato and Xenophon.

(7) The Penguin Classics, pp. 32, 35-37.

Matthew 3. 5.

When he was finally brought before the Supreme Court of Athens and sentenced to death for his Philosophy, this was his final statement:

"If you doubt whether I am really the

sort of person who would have been sent to this city as a gift from God, you can convince yourselves by looking at it in this way. 'Does it seem natural that I should have neglected my own affairs and endured the humiliation of allowing my family to be neglected for all these years, while I busied myself all the time on your behalf, going like

a father or an elder brother to see each one of you privately, and urging you to set your thoughts on goodness?

If I had got any enjoyment from it, or if I had been paid for my good advice, there would have been some explanation for my conduct; But, as it is, you can see for yourselves that although my accusers unblushingly charge me with all sorts or other crimes. there is one thing that they have not had the impudence to pretend on any testimony, and that I have ever exacted or asked a fee from anyone. The witness that I can offer to prove the truth of my statement is, I think, a convincing one

- my poverty." (8)

A man with these views and who defended them to death was a veritable saint and deserves veneration and the imitation of all who believe in the Primary of moral values.

These, your Lordships, are the views which, in all humility, I would like to put before you, on the occasion of the official founding of this historic institution of Sacred Studies in West Cameroon.

I say that in the running of it, from the beginning to the end, it should keep ever before its eyes the target which the ancient Irish Church set for itself in an age of primitive barbarism - the production of Saints and Scholars. Its future alumni should be instinct with charity, deep in knowledge, and steeped in genuine religion.

(8)

Plato: The Apology.

The Penguin Classics, pp. 43-44

The Seminary - a Veritable University

There is a prevalent attitude in secular circles which looks down on Seminary studies as inferior studies. And it must be said frankly that the missionaries, in Africa, put a premium on this contempt, by refusing to grant degrees to students after long years of book-worm drudgery. After three years of Philosophy and four years of Theo-logy, they came out with not a single internationally recognized title. And those who failed to become priests. after six years in the juniorate and seven years of Theology, were classified as primary school leavers, when it came to getting a job; while in Europe, a fellow who had spent such a substantial slice of life on books would have emerged with a Doctorate. In French-speaking territories, the imported anti-clericalism of the Intellectuals worsened the situation.

Here in Yaounde, if a G.C.E. holder comes with Scripture as one of his subjects, the thing is regarded as a big joke. They are blind to the fact that, as a literary and humanist work, the Bible ranks among the loftiest classics.

I studied for six years in the Seminary And about seven in several Universities.

And I have inside knowledge of both institutions; and I say that a well-staffed and organised Seminary is a veritable University; it Is even more, because it lays serious stress on Moral as well as on Intellectual Education; and in my mind, a thorough moral education takes the first place.

My firm conviction is that after three years of serious philosophical studies, a student who merits well should obtain a B.A. in Philosophy, and after his four years in Theology, a Bachelor in Divinity. They do that in Maynouth, in Ireland. Why not in Cameroon? I know what I am talking about; for having to begin University studies all over again, after leaving the Seminary, I had to start all from scratch; thus, I wasted seven precious years of my life and obtained, at thirty-six, what should have obtained at thirty years of age. No; a well-staffed and serious Seminary has nothing to envy from a secular academy.

To create a tradition of high standards, I believe that our Seminary should begin by affiliating itself to a well-established University abroad, while modifying its curriculum to suit African realities.

The yearly falling of standards in our institutes of learning, the mediocrity and the laissez-faire that are fast taking root in them, should be a warning to us in the running of this Seminary. It should

become an example for all to admire and imitate for its high standards of Learning and Discipline.

On this head, care should be taken to see to it that the right attitude and mentality and effort should be instilled, right from the start. No quarter should be given to a lackadaisical approach, on the part of all concerned, to things of such serious import.

Remember the time-tested adage in the stamping out of pernicious tendencies.

Principiis obsta: Kill the evil at its birth.

Remember too the wise and pertinent warning of Aristotle: **Parvus error in principio magnus est in fine**: a little error at the start attains staggering proportions at the end.

Bear ever in mind the weighty saying of the famous Dr. Aggrey of Ghana: Only the best is good enough for Africa.

The Salt of the Earth

When you see what dedication, what selfless kindness and generosity, what deep concern for human life and dignity, prevail in Mission hospitals, in schools and colleges, and in social services run by nuns and priests and brothers, black and white; when you have visited the unique centre which have visited which Cardinal of Montreal resigned his See and came to build in Cameroon out of his deep concern for handicapped children, you see what the Church can do in the uplift of the world, even in things secular.

What strikes you most is the total dedication, the spiritual conscientiousness, of those engaged in this noble work. If they were multiplied a hundredfold, the Church would become what Christ called it - the

Salt of the Earth. Authorities who do not appreciate this participation and are lukewarm or hostile, are guilty of unpardonable blindness. Rather, they should give every encouragement to this salutary enterprise, give all the aid, and facilitate to the maximum the solution of their problems.

If they encounter difficulties and misunderstanding, their zeal, far from diminishing, should be stirred up to greater effort and energy, for if men do not see and appreciate, God on high certainly does, and rich will be their reward.

If I have anything to say to our white collaborators on this head, it is that they should do all in their power to give the highest education and training to their African co-workers. to make them share responsibility, with a view that the Africans can take over in the near future.

The tragic example of Biafra should be a lesson to all.

This is a matter of the most urgent im-portance. The time has come when there should be black female doctors, university graduates, and principals of schools among the sisterhood.

Another point I would beg leave to put before you is this; there are certain people who, seeing what white priests have done in building of churches which are own hands, lament that the African clergy are

not able to do the same. Let them bear in mind that the days of pioneers were the days of pioneers. They had no choice but to build themselves. But to demand that of student priests today, with so many Cameroon engineers-a yearly growing number, and some of them fervent Catholics - is pushing the point too far.

A spectacular phenomenon in the Grassland Church today is the number of girls who flock to the sisterhood.

Would it not be a great idea for the Church to make the Brotherhood more attractive by giving those with that vocation possibilities to be trained as engineers, architects, and such? Just as the Church, thanks to the aid of foreign Catholic organizations, sponsors lay students to become future doctors in Catholic hospitals, can the same not be done to train architects and builders and electricians?

Of course, the priest should have a clear idea of the sort of Church to build, bearing

in mind the exigencies of developments in a liturgy inspired by African culture. I agree that the priest should be a practical man, capable of repairing his car, for instance.

But to demand that priestly studies, already so vast, should be surcharged with courses in Architecture and masonry, however laudable and plausible it may look, is an irrelevant aberration on the Cameroon of today.

Ave Crux, Spes Unica

My personal political creed is socialism or the extreme, left. it is my deep-seated conviction; for am inverately against a system which perpetuates abundance for the few and misery for the many. But I am a firm believer in the Catholic Church, which until the **Pacem in Terris** of John XXIII looked askance at even milder schools of Socialism. But see no contradiction in my stance.

Once in the Soviet Union, I asked a Russian writer this question: What is your quarrel with religion, since genuine religion stands for Social Justice, and so does Socialism? He gave me no answer! But I knew.

There is no intrinsic, inherent essential quarrel between Communism and Religion.

The quarrel is extrinsic, historical, and accidental. The Communist dubbed religion "the opium of the people" and ridiculed it for preaching

Pie in the sky

When you die,

precisely, as I have said before, because the Church allowed herself to be prostituted by materialism and made herself the ally, if not the lackey, of the monied classes; because she had often remained silent in the Face of blatant injustice. You are not unaware of the German play **The Vicar** which took the saintly and revered Pius XII to task for keeping mute, instead of speaking out, when Hitler was slaying the Jews. For my part, I have never read any-

where that the Church raised a voice against the extremely inhuman atrocities perpetrated on the Negro race, during four sombre centuries of slavery. And today, while the Portuguese are butchering black men in Africa, the Pope makes a pilgrimage to Portugal. It was a gesture which, in spite of its piety, hurt the heart of many a fervent African Catholic.

It is the Church which is largely responsible for the alienation of masses of peoples from herself.

Yet, these defects do not blind me to the inherent excellence of Religion, as an ideal in its purity. I am convinced that, if the Church were everywhere faithful to her mission, she would be an unparalleled power in the purification of man and the world.

And when I look at the world today, at its ravenous greed, at its rank materialism, at the heartless slaughter of millions, at the myriad glaring injustices, lam firmly convinced that Religion is the **Spes unica**, the only hope of man, I am firmly convinced that the Church, true to her ideals, dedicated to God, and firm in the right, is a tremendous power for the promotion of truth and goodness and justice on earth.

But pardon me if I say straight that I am no advocate of **Catholic Power**. Witness Portugal. Witness Spain. All die im- hard perialists. During my student days in Ire-land, back in the early fifties, I saw that Mr.

Costello's Government was dominated, and even sometimes brow-beaten into submission, by the Irish Hierarchy, even in affairs which were clearly non-ecclesiastical. It was a veritable dictatorship of the right. This assertion, by me, a man that owes all but the whole of his education to Old Ireland, may rouse the ire of some of my numerous Irish friends, and they would itch to join issue with me for saying this. Let them recall the famous affair of Dr. Noel Brown, a go-head Minister of Health, whose progressive programme, and whose brilliant career were crushed by a bench of reactionary Bishops. (9)

From what I have seen these many years, have made my own the slogan of an Irish Catholic patriot (I think it was John Dillon) who declared:

I take my religion from Rome, but my politics from home.

The Church's role is essentially a religious and moral one: to stand up for God against evil, for right against wrong, for humaneness against cruelty, for the dignity of man against his debasement, for heroism against cringing emasculation, for justice against injustice.

To wield this power, it needs a saintly, learned, and courageous clergy. And for this, the Seminary is the ideal School and should attain the highest levels in its aims.

Let me remind your Lordships that the lowering of standards in secular African institutes, the laissez-faire attitude towards discipline, the incitement to luxurious living, are part and parcel of the imperialist plot to keep the black man under and perpetuate his enslavement.

Oh! For a United Church

For a saintly, learned, and fearless clergy wield this power, there must be un-severable unity of mind and heart and will among the total body of the church's rulers, that is among the Episcopate and the Priesthood. The young seminarians, in despite of difference of temperament and mind, must be brought up in a veritable brotherhood, their hearts must be bound, in Christian love, by that

Fellowship of Kindred Minds

which a pious poet likened to the unity of the Trinity itself.

---

(9) For a detailed account on this question, I refer them to Paul Blanshard's factual, book: **The Irish and Catholic Power;** controversial Derek Verschoyle Limited, London, 1954.

Without the firmness of this unity, how can the Episcopate and the clergy become, as their very mission is to be, the natural guardians of genuine quality against the shoddy, of truth against falsehood, of good against evil, of charity against wickedness, of right rule against oppression, of justice against injustice, of faith against godlessness.

A worldly, ambitious, divided, factious, quarrelsome Episcopate and Priesthood is the greatest tragedy that can befall, not just the Church, but the people at large, and spells doom for a country where there are souls to be saved and wrongs to be righted.

That is why it must be dinned into the ears and instilled in the hearts and minds and wills of the cadet priests-to-be that the unity of the total clergy, in faith and charity and truth and right, makes the Church a very rock of strength. They must be made to realise that the priesthood is not a worldly career, but a sacred vocation, demanding selflessness, devotion and genuine dedication.

My Lords, as the Bible says:

"There is a season for everything, a time for every occupation under heaven:

A time for giving birth, a time for dying a time for planting

a time for uprooting what has been planted.

A time for killing, a time for healing; a time for knocking down, a time for building.

A time for tears, a time for laughter; a time for mourning, a time for dancing.

A time for throwing stones away, a time for gathering them up; a time for embracing,

a time to refrain from embracing.

A time for searching, a time for losing; a time for keeping, a time for throwing away.

A time for tearing,

a time for sewing;

a time for keeping silent, a time for speaking.

A time for loving, a time for hating;

a time for war, a time for peace.

What does a man gain for the efforts that he makes? I contemplate the task that God gives mankind to labour at. All that he does

Is apt for its time; but though he has permitted man to consider time in its wholeness man cannot comprehend the work of God from beginning to end.

But I still observe that under the sun crime is where law should be, the criminal where the good should be. 'God', I thought to myself 'will judge both virtuous and criminal, because there is a time here for all that is purposed or done.' " (10)

My Lords, your time has come to give birth, to plant and to build, to heal and to search, to gather and to sew; your time has come to speak.

I must beg your pardon for taking upon

Myself to lecture you, as it were, on a question that is, first and foremost, your own concern and responsibility. If the Second Vatican Council had not ordained that the laity should be, not only seen, but heard, in affairs touching the welfare of the Church, this initiative of mine would be frowned upon as unpardonable presumption, as overweening arrogance.

But I know that, imbued with the spirit of that Council, you will readily pardon me have gone beyond bounds.

But I have written this letter because I believe that the founding of the Senior seminary in your twin dioceses is a land-hark in the History of West Cameroon, a matter of the highest importance that should be of concern to all of us - Bishops, priests, laymen, and even to the people at large, whatever be their religious persuasions.

Ecclesiastes 3:1-11. 16.

We cannot afford to fail. We have no choice but to succeed, and succeed in the highest degree.

It is only thus that we can create a solid institution that will impose respect. It is only thus that we can create a sound, solid and lasting tradition of saintliness and scholarship. It is only thus that we can leave an example worthy of pride to those coming

after.

And believe me to be, my Lords,

Yours with deep respect.

Bernard Fonlon

Yaounde

Sunday, the 16th of September, 1973.